A Thousand Paths to Zen

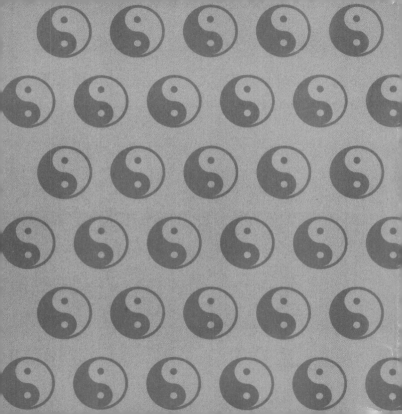

A Thousand Paths to
zen

Robert Allen

MQP

Contents

Introduction

Zen is a path to spiritual fulfillment. In order to follow it you need to be able to do two things: sit on your butt and breathe. How hard is that? Do you need to be a Buddhist to do Zen? No. Zen and Buddhism are kissing cousins but they aren't married. Any Christian, Jew, Muslim, or atheist can study Zen without compromising his or her beliefs. There are three things that will help along the way: great faith—not faith in a Christian sense but simply a firm belief that the Zen path will lead to enlightenment; great doubt—you must be prepared to take nothing for granted and examine everything for yourself from the ground up; and great perseverance—Zen is not instant enlightenment, it takes years of constant effort. Travel the path and enjoy!

This book contains a few terms you may not be familiar with so here are some words of explanation to help you along your way. *Satori* is the state of enlightenment. *Zazen* is Zen meditation. A *bodhisattva* is an enlightened person who, rather than entering nirvana, stays in the world to help others on their journey. You'll find mention of the Four Noble Truths, the Noble Eightfold Path, and the Precepts. Taken together these make up the Buddhist rules of behavior and are very roughly equivalent to the Ten Commandments.

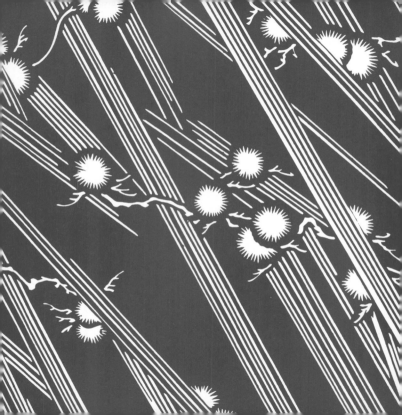

Seeds are
Planted

If you find yourself on a path to Zen be assured that you are going in the wrong direction.

There is nothing magical about Zen. You can see it right in front of you now.

Throw out opinions, prejudices, and theories until there is nothing left. Then throw out the nothing.

The study of Zen requires your constant and unwavering inattention.

If you go looking for Zen it will come looking for you.

Start on the journey and 10,000 bodhisattvas will spring up to guide your steps.

If you want to find Buddha, then Buddhism is an obstacle that must be overcome.

There are many strange things about the mind—for one, it has no outside.

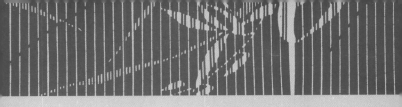

You will never understand Zen the way you understand algebra, but you might understand it the way you understand breathing.

Nirvana is not like heaven—you can't *go* there. All you can do is realize that you are there already.

Resist the temptation to pick the world up and shake it. Shake yourself instead.

In Zen there are no bad days. Every day is a good day.

Zen is not a Band-Aid. You can't simply apply it in an emergency. If you want what it can give, you must work for it now.

Your understanding is like a plum. When it is ripe it will fall from the tree of its own accord.

Zen is like lightning. There is no telling where it will strike. But if you want to be enlightened it's best to climb a tree.

Teachers can only open a door. You must walk through it under your own steam.

When you see a finger pointing to the moon, if you are wise you will look at the moon, not the finger.

Tread softly, live gently. That won't make you enlightened but it keeps you out of the worst of the mire.

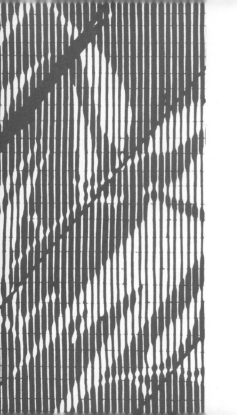

**Zen is not
a religion.
It is a way
of life.**

Like
poetry,
Zen uses
words to
say what
cannot
be said.

Buddha images are essential. Where else would you find such good paperweights?

Zen masters used to reinforce their lessons with blows. If this seems cruel, consider the lessons life teaches and the heavy blows with which they are hammered home.

A monk's robe is a uniform much like any other. Make sure you look at the wearer not the uniform.

If you stub your toe, don't curse. Just feel the Zen throbbing in your foot.

Like a drunk man falling over his own feet, you fall over Zen but struggle on without noticing.

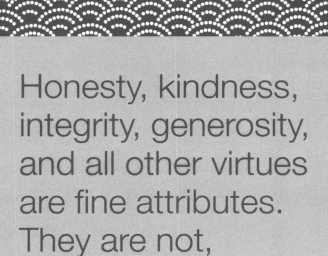

Honesty, kindness, integrity, generosity, and all other virtues are fine attributes. They are not, however, Zen.

A Zen student will improve in character and that is good. But never forget for a moment that the real purpose of your study is Zen itself.

Real Zen has no name. It is beyond all names. Anything that calls itself Zen, isn't.

If you are a Zen person there is no need to struggle. Zen will draw you the way a magnet draws iron filings.

The world is a received opinion and no one will thank you for questioning it. But that is what Zen is about.

A tree reaches for the sky because that is the nature of trees. Zen students reach for enlightenment because that is their nature.

If you feel special because you are studying Zen, you've missed the point. It is nothing special.

Smile! Like life, Zen is much too important to be taken seriously.

Some of the ancient masters were stern and tough, others were humorous, and others seemed quite insane. There is no one right way to do Zen.

If your house is your most important possession then it is your prison. Your house should be a hostel you happen to stay in day after day.

You begin by polishing your mind
to keep it safe from blemishes.
Later you realize that there is
nothing that can stain it.

Good teachers are rare. Make
sure that the teacher is good
for you rather than that you
are good for the teacher.

Zen seems impossible, and it is.
But even so you have to do it.

Be careful before you take up Zen. Once taken up it cannot be put down.

There are few good teachers nowadays, so when you meet others on the path, help them and let them help you.

You can search for Zen throughout the world but you will only find it here and now.

Look! Look! Look!
You still can't see it?
It's closer than the tip
of your nose.

Let everyone you meet be your teacher. There is no one who has nothing to give you.

Avoid those whose purpose is to drag you down. They hate anyone who will not roll in the mud with them.

Use all the muck in life to fertilize your flowers.

You don't believe in Zen?
If you didn't believe in
gravity could you fly?

Zen is not a career
move. It won't give
you power or prestige.

Nirvana is a gloomy Monday morning in January, when the car's broken down and the bus is late.

The masters of old were often homeless mendicants, but Zen still works if you've got two kids, a mortgage, and a car loan.

Zen is not a religion. If you took
Zen and ripped out its guts,
what is left would be a religion.

**Zen is not for people who
feel religious once a week.**

Zen is fine for those who
feel religious all the time.
They'll get over it.

Those who feel they are too hard-headed for such nonsense are too soft-headed to understand.

Before the first step is taken the goal is reached.

Mumon

In life we get busier and busier as time goes by. In Zen you do less and less. Eventually you do nothing, but nothing is left undone.

Just as all rivers lead to the sea, all people are drawn to Zen. They may not call it by that name or even know where they are going, but the call is irresistible nonetheless.

On the day you say, "At last I understand Zen!" you're in *real* trouble.

Some would move mountains by faith, but Zen leaves the mountains just where they are. It is not our business to rearrange the mountains.

People set out to change the world. What fools! Change yourself and the world will change of its own accord.

In meditation, if you itch, scratch, if you sneeze, wipe your nose. These things are also Zen.

Incense perfumes a room, but it stinks if you think it is anything holy.

Robes and bells are very nice if you like dressing up. They have nothing to do with Zen.

There are more statues
of Buddha than any other
man who ever lived.
Each and every one is an
obstacle to your progress.

Once you have started on the Zen path even if you give it up, it will never give up on you.

Imagine that you spoke a foreign language fluently but each day you forgot just a little. Day after day you unlearned all that you knew. That unlearning is Zen.

Flowers flourish knowing nothing of horticulture. Zen flourishes knowing nothing of philosophy.

Like a
mighty oak
tree your
Zen grows
slowly and
sturdily.

Don't fret and worry over Zen.

Don't waste hours thinking about what you should do.

Meditate and let Zen grow within you (and without you).

The reason you can't see Zen is because you're standing too close.

Zen is seen as confusing and difficult, but that isn't so. Our mind makes it that way because it is not used to dealing with such simplicity.

If your mind is full of unsatisfied desires, you'll never understand.

We are all like the drowning
man who clutches at straws.
Zen is like swimming lessons.

**Zen is plain, not fancy.
All complications serve to distract
you from the truth.**

A young mother complained to her teacher that looking after the baby left her no time for Zen meditation.
"Looking after a baby *is* meditation," he replied.

Here I stand, I can do no other. God help me. Amen.

Martin Luther

Now there was someone with an inkling about Zen.

Like climbing a mountain, Zen involves a great struggle. Eventually you will understand that the mountain is just another aspect of yourself.

Don't spend all your time thinking about God. It makes your brain ache and it lures you far from the path.

Doing evil is like rolling in muck. As long as you stop it's possible to scrub up.

According to Zen, not only will all people be saved, but even the grass and stones will become enlightened.

People ask, "What is the point of a religion like Buddhism that has no god and no heaven?"

Zen asks, "What is the color of the wind?"

Do good as long as you don't expect it to do *you* any good.

Just shut up for once and listen to the silence.

There is nothing wrong with religion as long as it doesn't get in the way of God.

Does Zen teach a belief in God? Yes. No. Don't know. Don't care.

Trying to understand Zen is like trying to relax. You just have to let it happen to you.

Morality is what religions teach when they've ceased to understand the point.

Reading about Zen is like reading about food. It's informative and fun but you can't live on it.

I hate it when people ask, "What is Zen?" It's like a fish asking, "What is water?"

In a world of "facts" and certainty, Zen offers us the gift of complete confusion.

You don't have to act Japanese to do Zen. It works just the same whether you're from Tuscaloosa or Cockfosters.

Zen is like traveling home in a fog. You _know_ the way even if you have trouble finding it.

To understand intimately one should see sound.

Mumon

You are enlightened already. Now you just need to know it.

A student said to his master, "There is one place in my mind that is always quiet and serene." "Quick!" cried that master, "Get rid of it!"

There's a Zen saying: "One inch time, one foot gem." Of course, doing nothing is a good use of your time.

For Buddhists, like so many others, information, study, and comment are endless. Yet none of these will yield the tiniest scrap of Zen.

You're too old to start Zen?
The master Joshu started when he was
sixty, became enlightened at eighty,
and taught for many years after that.

What was your
original face before
your father and
mother were born?

Koan

What is Zen?
Selling water
by a river.

**If you think of
enlightenment as
some kind of prize
that you can win,
you'll never get
there.**

Joshu asked,
"What is the Path?"
Nansen answered,
"Everyday life is the
Path."
"Can it be studied?"
asked Joshu.
"If you study it you'll
be far away from the
truth," came the reply.

Say you have an old rock you use as a paperweight. One day you drop it and, looking at the damage, you see the glint of gold. Suddenly that old familiar rock is transformed in your eyes. That is what your life is like when you find enlightenment.

Just like the patriarch Daruma you can meditate until your legs drop off, but without the right understanding it will do you no good at all.

People look for complexity in Zen because they cannot see the simplicity.

If someone thinks, "I am a good person," the idea gets in the way of the reality.

Zen that makes you miserable is not Zen. Buddhism that makes you a moralizing prig is not Buddhism. Nice and easy is the way.

Life and death are not two opposed things—they are two sides of a coin that isn't there.

People think they will find Zen in some wild, remote place. But they will only find whatever Zen they take with them.

You stand more chance of finding the abode of music in the body of a lute than of finding a soul in the body of a human being.

It is strange how Buddhist students so earnestly seek teaching, often traveling the world to find it, and then completely fail to see it staring them in the face.

Those who speak do not know. Those who know do not speak.

While alive,
become
dead, then
do what
you will,
all is good.

Bunan

No one owns Zen. It goes where it wants.

Watch your breathing carefully. How strange that such an ordinary thing can lead to Zen!

Who is the eye that sees?
Who is the mind that thinks?

**The master asked, "Who binds you?"
The pupil replied, "No one."
The master rejoined, "So why do
you seek liberation?"**

All those teachers,
eager to lead you
astray!

They say a goldfish has a memory span of three seconds, but at least he doesn't forget who he is.

You must want Zen as much as one whose head is held under water wants air.

I used to love Buddhist temples because they were holy. Now I love them because, to me, they aren't holy at all.

Green
Shoots
Grow

Let Zen be your life,
but do not let all your
life be Zen.

**If you don't understand
what you are told about
Zen, don't worry. One day
you'll say, "Oh, so *that's*
what they meant."**

Don't waste time learning the lotus position. Zen is not about stiff legs.

A flag waves in the wind. Does the flag move or does the wind move? Mind moves.

Those minimalist Japanese interiors that we admire so much tell you a lot about Japanese esthetics but nothing about Zen.

Fall down seven times but get up eight.

Zen is not a competition to see who gets enlightened first.

Even to speak the word *Buddha* is like being dragged through the mud, soaking wet. Even to say the word *Zen* is a complete embarrassment.

Blue Cliff Record

Three things are essential: great doubt, great faith, and great perseverance.

Let Zen soak you just as a heavy drizzle soaks your clothes.

In walking, just walk,
in sitting, just sit.
Above all, don't wobble.

Yun-men

**Not only can you not step twice
into the same river, *you* cannot step
twice into the same river.**

Jack Cohen

Philosophy merely talks about life. Zen *is* life.

Why is solitary confinement the worst punishment? Why are people so afraid to confront themselves?

Put this book down? Too late, you have Zen on your fingers.

If you study Zen prepare to be misunderstood.

If you could bottle Zen you'd never sell it. It would taste of clear water and smell of fresh air.

Your name is just a label you hide behind. What is your *real* name?

If you cannot find the truth right where you are, where else do you expect to find it?

Dogen Zenji

Is your hand your body or your mind?

When someone makes a silly, inconsequential remark and a friend says, "That's very Zen" — it isn't.

A student said, "I'd really like to get enlightened while I'm still young enough to enjoy it." Blockhead!

Spring comes and the grass grows by itself.

Zen saying

The mind is like water. Thrash around in it and you will only stir up the mud. Just let it settle of its own accord.

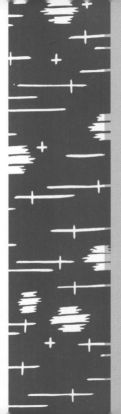

Try to get Zen and you will fail, but if you don't try you'll never get it.

Everyone knows that the shortest distance is as the crow flies, so why do they all take the long way around?

Miraculous power and miraculous activity,
Drawing water and hewing wood.

P'ang-yun

Buddha never said a word.

A pot is empty, yet that emptiness is the whole point of the pot.

Beyond, beyond, totally beyond, perfectly beyond: Awakening…Yes!

Heart Sutra

Your own nature is fundamentally clean and pure.

A girl is crossing the street, is she the younger or the older sister?

Koan

Some think that Zen is some kind of party game where you just have to say the first thing that comes into your head, but that's not it at all.

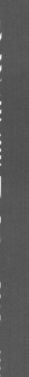

Zen is the gateless gate.

Eat, sleep, get up;
This is our world.
All we have to
do after that
Is to die.

Zen poem

It's not understanding Zen that takes the time, it's understanding all the things that aren't Zen.

Why do you want Zen? If you know, then you don't know.

If you are a real man you may drive off the farmer's ox or snatch food from the starving.

Yuan-wu

"He beat me, she tricked me, they laughed at me." If you think like this you'll never understand.

Everything the same, everything different.
Zen saying

There is no such quality as male and female. In its ultimate nature, every mind is the same.

Zen is one thing that gets much better as you get older.

A dog chasing its tail is no more foolish than a person searching for enlightenment.

The city of happiness is in the state of mind.

Should you desire great peace,
prepare to sweat white beads.

Hakuin

Zen is a journey.
The destination
is yourself.

**Whatever some say, meditation is
not a habit like cleaning your teeth.
You have to mean it.**

In
meditation
it is quality
not
quantity
that
counts.

Like the phoenix, when Zen is burnt it is reborn from the ashes.

Don't let anything distract you from your meditation. The distractions are the meditation.

In serving serve,
In fighting kill.

Jinzu

There is no path that leads to
Zen. How can you follow a path
to where you are right now?

Zen monks meditate with their eyes slightly open because what they are concerned with is right in front of them.

How many things I can do without!

Socrates

"What is Buddha?" a monk asked. "Dry dung," replied Ummon.

You see a great rock.
Is it inside or outside
your mind?

Zen question

**The emperor asked Daruma, "What
is the first principle of Zen?"
"Vast emptiness and nothing holy
anywhere," was the reply.**

Cover your path
With fallen pine
needles
So no one will
be able
To locate your
True dwelling
place.

Ikkyu

Learning Zen is a phenomenon of gold and dung. Before you understand it, it's like gold—after you understand it, it's like dung.

People talk of Zen-like calm. If only they knew how much sweat that calm has cost!

As one lamp serves to dispel a thousand years of darkness, so one flash of wisdom destroys ten thousand years of ignorance.

Hui-Neng

If your Zen seems like a high blank wall blocking a narrow alley, don't give up— find the magic word!

The obstacle is the path.

Zen saying

A monk who had struggled for liberation in vain for many years finally gave up and decided to devote the rest of his life to serving others with more aptitude for Zen. Instantly he was enlightened.

If you understand, things are just as they are—if you do not understand, things are just as they are.

Zen saying

You think that I am over here talking to you over there? Wrong.

As the blade of a sword cannot cut itself, as a fingertip cannot touch itself, so a thought cannot see itself.

Zen poet Seiken-Chiju spent twenty years on a pilgrimage only to realize he had not moved an inch.

The world is like a mirror. See? Smile, and your friends smile back.

Zen saying

To get rid of your passions is not nirvana—to look upon them as no matter of yours, that is nirvana.

Zen saying

In reality no one ever travels as much as an inch.

The wisdom of the world is no more than a refined form of stupidity.

To a mind that is still, the whole universe surrenders.

Chuang-Tzu

If you believe in God, you're mistaken. If you don't believe in God, you're mistaken. Agnostics, it goes without saying, are mistaken. Now, do you believe in God?

People say that Zen is contradictory. Well, it's not!

Do not seek the truth but cease to cherish opinions.

Zen saying

Have you seen that picture that looks either like two faces or one vase? Very Zen.

The world is ruled by letting things take their course.

Lao-Tzu

One day you'll think, "I'm beginning to understand." Beware that day.

What is the sound of one hand clapping?

Koan

Do not seek to follow in another's footsteps, rather seek what he sought.

A man who seeks revenge should start by digging two graves.

A flower falls, even though we love it; and a weed grows, even though we do not love it.

Dogen Zenji

At first I saw mountains as mountains and waters as waters. Then I saw that mountains are not mountains and waters are not waters. But now I have reached the essence of Zen and once again mountains are mountains and waters are waters.

Ch'ing-yuan

**Tame the wild
horse of your mind.**
Zen saying

How far will you
walk before you
admit it's the
wrong direction?

**Zen sweats the
small stuff.**

Why do you seek enlightenment when you already have your own treasure house?

Baso

A monk went to visit a dying friend.
"Shall I lead you on?" he asked.
"I came here alone and I go alone,"
was the reply.
"If you think you really come and go,
that is your delusion. Let me show
you the path on which there is no
coming and going." The monk
smiled and died.

Always remember that you reap just what you sow.

Seamless—
Touch it and it shimmers
Why use such nets
To catch sparrows?

                                        Gojusan

A mouse stealing rice grains from a barn knows more about Zen than you. At least the mouse knows what it needs.

Beware when the so-called sagely men come limping into sight.

Chuang-tzu

When an ordinary man acquires knowledge, he becomes wise. When a wise man attains enlightenment, he becomes ordinary.

Do what you like as long as you continue to seek enlightenment without cease.

Give up remembrance—
What end is there to pure
wind circling the earth?

Blue Cliff Record

The purpose of Zen training is not to help you understand but to demonstrate that you don't understand.

I only know that
I don't know.

Socrates

A bad person suffers like a
bad person. A good person
suffers like a good person.

The
Garden is
Cultivated

For twenty years I've
sought the Other.
Now, letting go,
I fly out of the pit.
What use oneness
of mind and body?
These days I only
sing la-la-la.

Keso Shogaku

Millions of Buddhas litter this world and every one of them's a fake.

Teaching people about Zen is as hard as teaching goldfish to juggle.

"While I was meditating," said the new student, "I saw a beautiful white bird come down and land on my head."
"Leaving you with feathers for brains," observed her teacher.

It used to be thought that poverty was the treasure of Zen. But that is not so. Even the affluent and comfortable, once bitten, feel Zen coursing through their veins.

A Zen student reached a wide river and, seeing his master on the far bank, called out, "Master, how do I get to the other side?"
"Fool!" shouted the master, "You're already on the other side!"

All beings by
nature are Buddha,
as ice by nature
is water;
apart from water
there is no ice,
apart from beings
no Buddha.

Hakuin

Plant a seed, let it germinate, then tend the plant. Zen is no more than this.

It's not hard to write a thousand pieces about what Zen is. But it's hellish hard to find anything to say about what it isn't.

I asked a child, walking with a candle,
"Where does the light come from?"
Instantly he blew it out. "Tell me
where it's gone and I'll tell you where
it came from."

Hasan of Basra

Buddhism is something that Zen trod in.

Refine your life as you would smelt
gold. Chuck out all the dross — then
you'll see how the dross and the gold
are the same thing.

There is nothing, nothing at all you can do that will cut you off from Zen. The worst you can do is to look the wrong way for a while.

Don't frown, Zen makes you feel better, not worse.

When you give to the poor, remember that it helps them not you.

You don't climb up to Zen, you sink into it.

It is as impossible for a Zen student to imagine life without Zen as it is for most people to imagine a life without breathing.

Life is an opinion.

The only way to teach anyone anything worth learning is by example.

Don't waste one moment on your past mistakes. All flowers need manure.

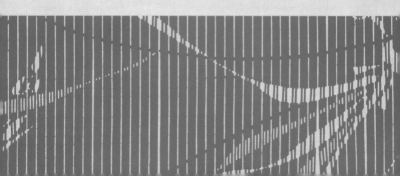

As long as you seek enlightenment you will never see that you already have it.

Zen masters often hit their pupils. When life smacks you across the head bow and say, "Thank you."

Trying to explain to beginners is called "grandmotherly kindness" — it is well intentioned but often does more harm than good.

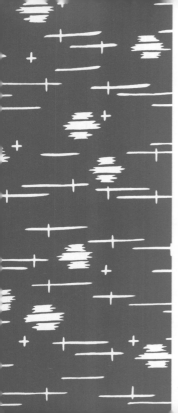

People who know
nothing of it try
to discuss Zen.
What idiots! How
can you discuss
your nose?

**Like Daruma,
you can sit facing
a wall for years
but without
understanding,
it will do you no
good at all.**

There was a Zen master so strict that he always slept sitting up and even died in that position. Did he think Zen is so weak it can't work lying down?

It's amazing how well dead men can teach Zen.

Tea is just this:
First you make the water boil,
Then infuse the tea.
Then you drink it properly.
That is all you need to know.

Sen-No-Rikyu

People ask me,
"What is Zen like?"
It's green.

A certain writer wrote of
an incense that he called,
"The very essence of Zen."
Obviously he'd never
smelled rotten tomatoes.

Once you have breathed Zen it will, like oxygen, reach every part of your body.

If you gaze for long into the abyss, the abyss also gazes into you.

Nietzsche

People talk about mind and matter. We know where mind is but where is matter?

Have you noticed that people who are
not getting paid will work harder and
more happily than those who are?
The mind is a strange place.

**An opinion is like
a bone in an egg.**

Those who cling to life die,
and those who defy death live.

Uyesugi Kenshin

The Emperor
asked Daruma
about Zen.
He pulled out
a flute, blew
a single note,
bowed, and left.

Zen is not as easy as falling off a log,
it's as easy as *not* falling off a log.

If you want excitement set
fire to your pants.
Zen isn't about excitement.

Some people call Zen a "Way of
Liberation," which sounds very impressive,
but who is to be liberated, and from what?

The last thing many people want to know is themselves.

In a church you uncover your head (unless you're a woman). In a mosque or a synagogue you keep your head covered. In a Buddhist temple you take off your shoes. And Zen? The sky is blue, the grass is green.

A sneeze!
What a great Zen
moment that was!

To be in a state of *satori* is to
be with God before he said,
"Let there be light."

D.T. Suzuki

You say far more about Zen when you keep your big mouth shut.

Washing the dishes is not only an excellent Zen exercise, but you get clean dishes too.

Someone suggested sarcastically that I should teach Zen to a soccer team to improve their performance. Good idea! At least soccer players have the sense to keep their brains in their feet.

Bitten by fleas and lice,
I slept in a bed,
A horse urinating all the time
Beside my pillow.

Basho

The enlightened person is not above karma but lives in accord with karma.

Master mind, do not be mastered by mind.

Zen saying

There is more Zen in a cup of tea than in all the scriptures put together.

Zen isn't the answer to all your problems—Zen *is* all your problems.

Zen isn't for everyone. It doesn't seek converts or make promises. If you think it's the path for you, that's fine. If not, find another path.

Reason is a fine tool. So is a hammer. Try building a house with just a hammer.

It's so odd that it takes years for people to learn to sit quietly and do nothing special.

All fundamentalists, whether theists or rationalists, build a prison and invite you to share it with them.

Zen people follow the path, not through desire for enlightenment or fear of death, but because they are made that way and have no choice.

You can do anything at all while you search for Zen, but Zen will still color you like a bright dye colors cloth.

Oh snail
Climb Mount Fuji,
But slowly, slowly!

Issa

Mind let alone will clear of its own accord. Mind is naturally clear and is clouded by wrong effort.

People call Zen "Eastern mysticism," so what do they call a loaf of bread?

When you learn to meditate there is no you, there is no Zen, and there is no meditation.

Zen is like one of those Japanese swords. Just a razor sharp cutting edge and everything else no more than decoration.

There are millions of hells and heavens, but not one is worth bothering with.

Just follow your breath. Watch it rise and fall. Too easy? But this is the key!

Bad people, good people, clever people, stupid people—far too much thinking!

My daughter bakes Zen cookies. I never tell her because, once she knew, she couldn't do it.

Without enlightenment you cannot save even yourself. When you become enlightened you save the whole world.

The master Joshu was asked whether a dog has Buddha nature. Buddhists believe that all creatures have Buddha nature but Joshu answered, "No" (Mu). What is Mu? This is one of the basic koans of Zen.

Just because you can't see the sun,
do you doubt that it's shining away
behind the clouds?
Zen is there whether you know it or not.

**Once upon a time you had to scour
the Far East to find Zen. Now,
thanks to modern communications,
you can get it delivered.**

Living with Zen is hard, living without it much harder.

A western Zen student wrote to friends to tell them that his local group had closed down. Apparently the members found they had too many important commitments.

Zen is like swimming. Don't struggle! You were designed to float.

Thinking, talking, or reading about Zen are OK, but if you want to get anywhere you have to do Zen.

It's fun to know about things as long as you don't treat your knowledge very seriously. It's when you think that it actually counts for something that you wind up in trouble.

Zen is not instead of thinking, it comes before thinking.

Buddhism and Zen may be kissing cousins—but they are not married.

Everyday people ask, "Where is Zen?" just at the moment they trip over it.

There are no paths—you must trample the undergrowth for yourself.

People who meditate often worry that they aren't "doing it right." If you keep doing it, one day you'll do it right.

I like Zen because it tickles.

People ask, "What is enlightenment?"
To understand the answer you'd have to understand the question.

To live at all is miracle enough.

Mervyn Peake

Buddhism, like all major religions, seeks to eliminate evil and promote good. Zen goes straight for the jugular.

The Indians passed it to the Chinese, who passed it to the Japanese, who spread it all over the world. It must be the only time the Japanese resisted the urge to miniaturize something.

It's funny how people thirst for magic and miracles, then resolutely look the wrong way when they happen.

"How does Zen work?" people ask. It doesn't work.

Buddha held out a flower and one of his disciples, Maha Kasyapa, smiled—the first koan was solved.

The modern master Shunryu Suzuki said that *satori* is like having children. Before you have them it seems like a miracle, but afterward it just seems natural.

People see some raked gravel, read a couple of *haiku*, and think they know what Zen is. If they can't find it in their local shopping mall they have no idea what it is.

Meditation creeps up on you like wine. One minute you can't feel the difference and the next you can't feel your legs.

People try to enter Zen by pushing at the door marked "Pull."

All religions, with the best of intentions, obscure the truth because it is so hard to explain. Zen makes it seem hard because no one can grasp how simple it is.

When you sit in meditation, heaven and hell are shaken to their foundations.

What are you so feverishly running after? Putting a head on top of your own head, you blind idiots? Your head is right where it should be. The trouble lies in not believing in yourselves enough.

Lin-chi

Mind and body dropped off; dropped off mind and body! This state should be experienced by everybody—it is like piling fruit into a basket without a bottom...however much you pile you cannot fill it up.

Dogen

On returning from China to Japan the enlightened Dogen was asked what he had learned:
"I have come back empty-handed. I have realized only that the eyes are horizontal and the nose vertical."

The great master Lin-chi, founder of the Rinzai school of Zen, had the following inscription over his door:
He who holds that nothingness
Is formless, flowers are visions,
Let him enter boldly!

The illiterate peasant Hui-neng, who was to become one of Zen's greatest masters was enlightened when one day he overheard someone recite:
"Depending on nothing you must find your own mind."

The only person stopping you from being enlightened is you.

An enlightened person could no more teach you enlightenment than Pavarotti could teach you to sing like him.

The path is broad, but people do not tread it because they don't know where it leads.

"We want God! We want enlightenment! We want peace!"
Oh, shut up and eat your meal.

When you can breathe with your ears and see with your nose you will be enlightened.

Daruma's Zen is not yours,
Hakuin's Zen is not yours,
Lin-chi's Zen is not yours.
Do not rely on great masters
but find your own Zen.

Once, if you wanted Zen, you would find a master and become his disciple. Now it's not that easy. What will you do—give up? No, put on stout shoes and follow your own path.

While you don't get the point,
all the scriptures in the world
won't help you.
When you do get the point—
who needs scriptures?

Who is the seer who sees?
Who is the thinker who thinks?
These are the things you must
understand.

Just sitting on your butt, breathing in and out—how hard can that be?

Meditation takes you to some beautiful places. Make sure you leave them behind.

Bliss is just the other side of despair—throw them both away.

Even if you accept the Four Noble Truths of Buddhism, keep the precepts to the letter, and follow the Noble Eight-fold Path, you will be not one inch nearer to enlightenment.

No one knows Zen. Even the enlightened masters have not the slightest idea what it is. It cannot be grasped by understanding—it can only be invited in.

A Japanese girl called Satsume experienced an awakening while still only in her teens. One day her father found her seated on one of the scriptures meditating and scolded her for her disrespect. "How," she replied, "does this scripture differ from my butt?"

Even the greatest master
never taught one word of Zen.

**Even in the depths of winter the
trees bear spring blossoms.**

Zen isn't about sitting quietly,
you need to be able to hold it
while you run for a bus.

**The gardeners have gone away
but Zen still blooms unaided.**

Look at a nut and you see the outside. Crack the shell and you see a new outside. Split open the kernel and you see two new outsides. Zen is on the inside of the outsides.

A Zen master accused Ummon of becoming a heretic. "Even if that is so," he replied, "it is sufficient to have obtained peace of mind."

I do not teach, I learn. If you can learn anything from me, then good luck to you.

Wham! Just like that a hawk seizes a sparrow.

Those who stole Zen have fled and left it lying around so people can fill their pockets.

When Zen is after you, you can run but you can't hide.

"Work hard! Do hard training! Struggle with all your might!" That isn't Zen—it's aerobics.

Zen requires discipline but, sadly, some people are keener on the discipline than they are on the Zen.

If you are born for Zen you'll recognize it as soon as you meet it, even if you don't know the word or understand the first thing about it.

Understanding deepens slowly, like learning to play an instrument.

Sometimes Zen is like riding a tiger. Later you become the tiger.

Westerners like Buddhism because it cares about even the smallest creatures. But Zen is about more than fluffy kittens and cuddly bunnies.

Don't just sit there meditating.
Work is also part of the training.

Do not study Zen just to escape your everyday problems. Those problems *are* Zen.

To live a moral life is good,
but you cannot *deserve* Zen.

Because Zen is hard to grasp people think it doesn't exist. Do you refuse to believe that air exists just because you can't see it and grab a handful?

Dig, dig, dig—the answer isn't outside.

As long as you can see an inch of space between "this" and "that" you will not understand.

Wise men full of their own clever chatter may seem seductive, but they block your path like an avalanche.

Imagine that you were suddenly homeless. Would you still be interested in Zen?

Splash your face with cold water. That's your prayers for today over with.

Russia, according to Churchill was "a mystery wrapped in a mystery inside an enigma." Zen is the opposite.

If it has occurred to you to wonder why you want Zen then you probably don't want it enough.

A day without work is a day without food.

Hyakujo

If you avoid people you do not understand, how will you ever learn?

Bad people are Buddhas too. This is hard to understand which is why it is important.

To know
the answer,
first you
must lose
yourself
in the
question.

Weeds are
Pulled

Like gray hairs Zen grows on you with age. Unlike gray hairs you have to work for it.

Zen isn't what you believe, it's what you are.

The words of all the Zen masters of the ages stink like rotting corpses.

Make a nice big fire, chuck all your Buddhism on it, and warm yourself in its glow.

An old lady of great Zen insight was asked about the sound of one hand clapping. "Rather than bother with that," she said, "clap both hands and get on with it."

Life is 99.9 percent nonsense. The rest is Zen.

Religion stinks of righteousness and musty prayer books. Zen stinks of incense. Let's go out and breathe the fresh air.

When you make tea make tea, and when you make water make water.

The notes I handle no better than many pianists. But the pauses between the notes—ah, that is where the art resides!

Artur Schnabel

We all come out of "nothing" and go back to "nothing." Whatever this nothing is, it seems remarkably active.

Like hypochondriacs, when we think we're sick it's all in the mind.

Anyone who tells you, "I am enlightened," isn't.

The trouble with Buddhas is that they have a beatitude problem.

I've had more "spiritual" experiences mowing the lawn than I ever had in any church or temple.

Zen has a habit of clipping you around the ear just when you least expect it.

"And who are you?" said he.
"Don't puzzle me," said I.

Laurence Sterne

What a fool to struggle so hard to express in words that which is inexpressible!

When you first meet Zen it is like bumping in to your long-lost identical twin.

You must be able to feel Zen from the ends of your hair right down to your toenails.

Zen cannot be ignored. Like a fishbone in your throat, once you have it you have to do something about it.

A Zen monk asked his master,
"What would you give to a poor man?"
"He lacks nothing," came the reply.

The more you look for Zen
the more it isn't there.

**Shunryu Suzuki likened meditation
to baking bread over and over
again. He also said that once you
know one thing thoroughly, you
know all things.**

A man travels the world in search of what he needs and returns home to find it.

George Moore

Zen implies no-Zen, Buddha implies no-Buddha, and God implies no-God— do away with names, go beyond dualism. The true name has no name.

I once tried looking at a flower to see what Maha Kasyapa saw when Buddha showed him a flower and he became enlightened. I couldn't see a thing—right flower, wrong eyes.

People who laugh at Zen do no harm, they just don't understand. If they didn't laugh it wouldn't be Zen.

Even the most mundane life is a continual search for enlightenment. We may not know what we want, but we are quite sure, somewhere in the depths of the mind, that we want it.

A drunk finds his way home, even if he has no idea how he got there. We find our way to enlightenment with similarly faltering steps because that, also, is our home.

Savor your life. Chew every mouthful thirty times. If you rush you will miss something remarkable.

It is only when you are prepared to look at everyday life with fresh eyes that you will start to see what it is really about.

Not seeking enlightenment is *much* tougher than working strenuously to find it. For the idle there is no choice.

When you meditate do not expect miracles or magic, but expect (slowly, slowly) to see everyday life as it really is.

People who start to meditate think, "How boring! How itchy! I could be doing something useful!" Be patient. Sit quietly and watch. Something beautiful is being born.

Meditation is not about cutting yourself off from the world, but opening yourself up to it.

To begin with your life is divided into meditation and not-meditation. Later you realize that *everything* is meditation and not-meditation at the same time.

Be in no hurry to think yourself enlightened. If you think it, then you aren't.

Don't try to convert all your friends to Zen. There's nothing as tiresome as a missionary. But if you impress them with your own life, they might seek enlightenment for themselves.

Let Zen wear you smooth, like water dripping on rock.

What is the problem? I am the problem. Get rid of "I" and suddenly, no problem.

How can I get rid of "I." Ah, now that *is* a problem.

Many people are scared of meditation, like children frightened of the dark. How odd! Like a snail being scared of its shell.

Buddhism teaches that we seek enlightenment to escape the pain of endless birth and death. More likely we seek it just because it is our true nature.

We are like the Man in the Iron Mask. We long to see our true face but don't know how to unlock the mask.

If you allow yourself you will gravitate toward enlightenment naturally.

Like someone who falls into a river, people will clutch at anything to stay afloat.
The truth is, you can swim.

Zen is nobody's property, no one can give it to you or keep it from you—it is open to all.

In Zen there is no such thing as a day off. Zen keeps happening to you whether you want it to or not.

Zen is easy,
it's people who
are difficult.

Zen contradicts no one. There are many paths and ultimately even the "wrong" ones are right.

If Zen made sense you would at once be misled.

As long as you can find one solid place on which to rest a foot you have not found Zen.

Zen isn't about pie in the sky, it's about pie in the oven.

Will much meditation lead to enlightenment? Yes—though not on its own.

The more you try to hurry Zen the longer it takes. Can you hurry the growth of an oak tree?

Why bother about Zen at all? If you are a Zen person you already know why.

Zen does not speak but it certainly kicks.

Zen detached from Buddhism is like a horse freed from its cart. Watch it kick up its hooves as it runs free in the fields!

When you meditate the world becomes like warm molasses.

Meditation is often so wonderful that you wish you never had to stop. But this isn't the point. Don't do it for the nice feeling it gives, just do it for itself.

If you have Zen you'll never want for anything else.

There's nothing in this world that you can cling to. But how hard it is to let go!

With Zen you feel, like Socrates, that there are so many things you can do without.

Do as much good as you can, but
do not be attached to doing good.
It is not an aim in itself.

**If you make enlightenment
the aim of your Zen practice
you are wide of the mark.**

Just as you are only dimly
aware of yourself growing
older, you may fail to see your
Zen wisdom deepening.

The only person in the whole world you can change fundamentally is you.

Surely Zen should concern itself with helping other people? But there *are* no "other" people.

Be compassionate to the poor, the hungry, the homeless, and the persecuted, but don't get hooked on compassion—you have a job to do.

Don't be so keen to know things—it's *not* knowing that matters.

Is your consciousness inside your brain or is your brain inside your consciousness?

Can you tell someone how to ride a bike? Of course not, they have to feel it in their muscles and nerves. You have to feel Zen, too.

People are keen to keep their Zen going twenty-four hours a day. How do they think it could possibly stop?

Don't expect to understand
Zen like a piece of
conventional knowledge.
It's more like when you get
the point of a joke.

Don't think about
Zen, just inhale
deeply.

Don't be afraid of stepping off the path—your footsteps are the path.

In meditation the trick is to relax totally without falling asleep. Zen lives right next to the place where sleep is found.

Above you on the mountain are other climbers. If one yells back, "This stone is slippery!" make sure you pay attention.

Don't lose any time regretting what is past. You have a mountain to climb.

Like an apple I am Zen all the way to the core.

Some people strain at their meditation, trying desperately to find the answer. Sit quietly and let the answer come of its own accord.

Be still and watchful like a frog waiting for flies. The frog is no great hunter, he lets the flies do all the work for him.

There are no
vacations from Zen.
Once you start you
never stop.

**Trying to make Zen clear only leads
to complications. Let it sink in just
as it is and it will soak right through
you to the bone.**

If you want a quiet, meditative life, avoid Zen.

Zen is nothing more than your own true nature. Anything more would be gilding the lily.

Buddhist philosophy, psychology, and literature are all fascinating but, if it's Zen you want, you're better off without them.

People who think that Zen is some New Age fad are mistaken. It is so old that no one knows where it came from or what its name was.

Zen has no dogma or beliefs of its own. It is accessible to followers of any religion or none at all.

Does Zen promise an afterlife? No, but it does away with death.

Zen does not mention God because, if it did, people would be misled.

Once you embrace Zen your traveling is ended. Ever after, you will be in the here and now.

It is only when you get right up close that you begin to see what Zen looks like.

When Zen came west it slipped its leash. Now catch it if you can!

Why sit behind monastery walls looking for Zen when it's right here?

If all the Buddhas and patriarchs appeared before you right now, they could not give you Zen, nor could they take it from you.

Don't bother thinking beautiful, holy thoughts—flowers grow better in dung.

People that start meditation think it's boring. But just because you sit in the cockpit of a plane doesn't mean you know how to fly it.

There is a saying that water that is too pure has no fish.

People who meditate long for "something to happen." Did you ever learn a language or a musical instrument? Do you remember a moment when you could suddenly do it? The ability builds up slowly.

People used to think I was stupid when I talked about Zen. Now I get paid for it and they think I'm clever.

Fools regard themselves as awake now, so personal is their knowledge.

Chuang-tzu

When asked a question a Zen student might strike the floor or shout "Kwatz!" But this is only the answer if it comes from the depths of your understanding.

A bird eats crumbs of Zen and spreads white blobs upon the table.

It is said that when the pupil is ready the teacher appears. Of course, you have to recognize the teacher.

Anyone can teach you about Zen even if they don't intend to. You just have to be awake enough to receive the lesson.

Those who see black and white, good and evil, will never begin to understand Zen.

Those who see in endless shades of gray miss the point.

Let's stop yakking about Zen and go out and *do* it.

The Tree Flourishes

Just spread out a mat
For lying quite flat
When thought's tied to a bed
Like a sick man growing worse
All karma will cease
And all fancies disperse
That's what is meant by
enlightenment!

Ch'ing Ming

Emotions such as hate, greed, lust, and envy make lumps in your thinking. Even "good" emotions like love do the same. These lumps block the mind like clots in the blood block the arteries.

Sometimes the lumps in your thinking are small and dissolve easily. But sometimes they come back again. They can get bigger, too. What started out as tiny crystals can become pebbles, stones, and even boulders.

People who become obsessed by hate or anger or lust end up with whole mountains blocking their thinking.

When you see the lumps appearing in your mind, try to let them dissolve of their own accord. And, above all, don't encourage them to grow. Do you *want* a mountain in your mind?

Religions control people to make them behave in a certain way. Zen sets people free to behave just like people.

In Zen the universe is not good or bad. It is just as it should be with nothing added.

Is it dangerous to let people be themselves? Won't they steal, rape, and murder? But they do all that (often in the name of religion) anyway.

People cling tenaciously to their unhappiness. Why are the prisoners' chains so comforting when the door to the cell lies open?

To train yourself in meditation is to be a sitting Buddha. You should know that Zen is neither sitting nor lying…If you adhere to the sitting position you will not attain the principle of Zen.

Huai-jang

As children we are taught "life = good, death = bad." Do you really think they are different?

Even the most perfect life must end. Would you die without knowing the secret of life?

In Zen all hells and heavens are possible, but all are impermanent. Kick down hell, turn your back on heaven. Who needs them?

Few can get enough of life. Very few would turn down another chance. But that is because they don't understand what life and death are all about.

People love positive thinking. All that "you can do it if you only try" seems so inspirational. But do what, exactly? And why? Do you really think all that puff and sweat is going to change anything?

Just sitting, breathing in and out, may seem so plain, so pointless. But try it. Don't sit making shopping lists or re-fighting arguments in the office. Just let your mind go.

Zen won't make you rich and famous, it's *far* better than that.

I just cleared the garage. Threw out a dozen bags of garbage. Made three trips to the dump. What a Zen day!

Keep it simple, stupid!
This is very good Zen advice.

I saw a monkey
get down from
a tree in one
smooth, fluid
movement.
No "put this paw
here and that
paw there."
Wow, a Zen
monkey!

Westerners think it's cool to be able to eat with chopsticks. What's more important—being cool or getting the food into your mouth? Zen is about eating with your fingers.

Take it easy. You're not the one driving the train, you're just a passenger.

Just discard all [the knowledge] you have acquired as being no better than a bed made for you when you were sick.

Huang-po

Give up those thoughts that lead to false distinctions! There is no "self" and no "other." There is no "wrong desire," no "anger," no "hatred," no "love," no "victory," no "failure."

Huang-po

Don't fill your head with Zen, that's just a way to get a headache. Empty it of Zen and you'll truly have Zen.

Sartre used to talk about people being in the condemned cell. If you believe it, of course, it becomes true.

Zen is not instant. You can't just mix it with hot water and have enough for a family of four. You have to work at it patiently and prepare as though you were cooking a banquet for important guests.

Stop the booming of the distant bell.
Koan

You can't be truly religious and continue to believe in God.

Who dost thou prate of God?
Whatever thou sayest of Him is untrue.

Eckhart

Once you have run out of all ideas, including the idea of having no idea—that is Zen.

Talking about Zen is like talking about sex—not as great as the real thing.

Zen isn't an option— it's a compulsion.

The world is ultimately unknowable. Zen tells us so and science, by struggling unsuccessfully to prove the reverse, confirms that it's true.

Don't struggle to be a "someone." Realize that you are no one.

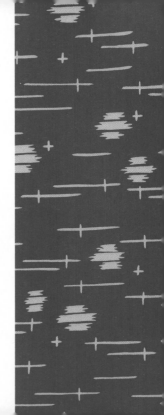

There is no end to learning. Knowledge is inexhaustible. These things are delightful but eventually they prove futile.

To disprove the theory that "it's all in the mind," Dr. Johnson kicked a rock as hard as he could. Where did the blockhead think the pain was?

Zen isn't hard—it's impossible. Yet people do it, and that's the attraction.

Zen is like swimming—when you give up trying you can do it.

Once you have tasted Zen, life without it would be as unthinkable as life without air.

Some people practice Zen meditation just for its health benefits, and some "serious" Zen students get very sniffy about this. Why? The moment you sit in *zazen* you'll go the whole way, sooner or later, like it or not.

Behold but One in all things. It is the second that leads you astray.

Kabir

A well-known academic once criticized Zen because, "anyone who has read a couple of paperbacks could be an expert on it." He saw this as the unforgivable sin.

Zen requires a certain style of thought. Some are born with it, some acquire it, and some hate the sight of it.

You don't have to believe in Zen, you just have to do it.

If you have no patience with "Eastern mysticism" then you may be surprised to find that Zen doesn't either.

Everyone starts out with their own idea of what Zen is all about. They are all wrong, but it doesn't matter—being wrong is one step on the path to the truth.

Drugs may convince you that you've glimpsed God—Zen introduces you.

Zen may look peaceful but don't study it if you want a quiet life. Zen is a revolution in your mind.

If you can breathe you can do Zen. It's really that simple.

To start there are Zen days and non-Zen days. When you have studied for a while you realize that the whole week is Zenday.

Eat when you're hungry, sleep when you're tired.

Zen saying

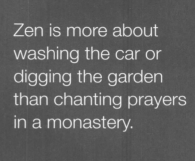

Zen is more about washing the car or digging the garden than chanting prayers in a monastery.

Liberating yourself from evil is not so hard. Discarding the idea of "goodness" is much harder.

Nothing on earth is so badly, wrongly, and irresponsibly taught as religion. God should sue.

Every church, temple, synagogue, and mosque is a monument to humanity's desire to ignore God.

If you had a friend who sent you a post card from Hawaii, would you know all about the place? That is just how much religions can tell you about God.

Sit quietly and listen carefully.
No, don't listen for the voice of God,
but for a special sort of silence.

**Eventually even the grass and
stones will become enlightened.**

Zen saying

People always like to think that God is
on their side. Zen is on no one's side.

The beginner's mind is like a dusty attic full of junk. Just sweep the whole place clean. There, isn't that much better?

Later you see that there was never any attic, no dust, and no junk.

We all walk on crutches, at least mentally. We lean upon things because we are afraid to walk on our own. Zen is about learning to throw the crutches away.

Zen is not escapism or quietism, it's about getting in there with reality.

A dog wanted a drink but was afraid of the other dog he saw in the water. Eventually he was so desperate that he leapt at the "other" dog and quenched his thirst.

To nurture your Zen you must learn to look at the world with new eyes. Take nothing for granted but look at what is really there.

Zen masters talk about doubt growing until it feels as if your mind is locked in ice, and then, just as you feel totally bewildered, the ice shatters and enlightenment dawns.

Zen is like food straight from the oven, too hot to eat but too delicious to leave.

Books cannot give you Zen any more than a travel book gives you a good vacation. Eventually you must make the journey yourself.

There are many tales of monks enduring untold hardships to discover Zen. But it is the discovery that matters, the hardship is extra.

Why climb Everest? Because it's there. Why do Zen? Same reason.

Zen doesn't make sense.
But then life is under no
obligation to make sense.

**You may feel that your Zen is
making no progress. All that is
barring your road is the idea of
being stuck. Let go of that *idea*
and you will proceed unhindered.**

It is said that Zen is like crossing
a river and reaching the opposite
shore with every step we take.

Speak of Zen and you lie.
Do not speak of Zen and you
fail to tell the truth.

**Psychology constructs theories
about the nature of Mind, while
Zen seizes it by the throat.**

Sitting and thinking about
Mind is as much good as
trying to tickle yourself.

God doesn't speak through priests, monks, theologians, or any other purveyors of religious wisdom. If you want God you have to go to the horse's mouth.

**A mind to search elsewhere
For the Buddha,
Is foolishness,
In the very center of
foolishness.**

Ikkyu

The Zen master Dogen said that good teaching should feel like something being forced on you— but that is only ordinary teaching. Good teaching feels like coming home to warm slippers.

Buddha, like an overzealous puppy, is forever under your feet.

No part of life should be ignored by the Zen student. Gulp the whole thing down or how will you know how it tastes?

Monks dread sex, hate music, despise frivolity. Any Zen that cannot encompass such things is a poor, weak, weedy little thing.

Zen was held captive by Buddhists who thought it was their private discovery. But Zen needs no Buddha, no teaching, and no monks. It is not like the tiger whose dwindling numbers are kept safe in captivity—it thrives in the wild and breeds all the time.

I obtained not the least thing from unexcelled, complete awakening, and for this very reason it is called unexcelled, complete awakening.

The Vajracchedika

Better to spend time with a prostitute than a prophet.

My Zen is not all bamboo and lotus blossoms. I prefer earth and worms.

Wealth, success, and possessions are supposed to be the great aims of life, but they change people only for the worse.

Talk to famous people. They see the world only through the rose-tinted glasses of their fame. How absurd! Do they think life cares about such trivia?

Instead of collecting money you might as well collect manure. At least flowers and bugs can thrive on manure. What eats money?

Just as you never see much from a freeway, you won't see much of life if you rush through being busy and successful. Take some time to wander down the country lanes of life and you might see what it's all about.

Some Zen teachers like to collect followers. A lot of followers must mean that the teacher is good. But no, a good teacher should need to be dragged unwillingly to the lecture hall.

Zen is such a nice, attractive word, but it *really* needs to go. It just gets in the way all the time.

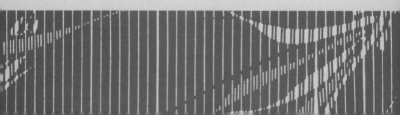

A famous Buddhist once said that you need to be able to, "get down in the gutter with a drunken prostitute." The thought of him actually doing it still raises a smile.

You can keep your Buddhism and your Zen. I'll just sit right here and watch sparrows.

When someone asked Yun-men what was the ultimate secret of Zen he replied, "Dumpling!"

All that incense— so good for keeping mosquitoes at bay.

A monk sat, saffron robe drawn around him tightly to show not an inch of flesh except his shaven head. Oh, how I longed to smack that shiny dome!

Of the enlightened man Zenrin said: Entering the forest he moves not the grass; Entering the water he makes not a ripple.

To save life it must be destroyed, When utterly destroyed, one dwells for the first time in peace.

Zenrin

There is nothing that is outside
Zen. And inside it is empty.

**There is no answer to a *koan* —
but you *must* answer. Whatever you
say, whatever you do, is wrong.
So what do you do? Answer! Now!**

"Not this! Not this!" —
the instruction of Zen
teachers through the ages.

People think of Zen as a branch of religion. It is time it was also a branch of psychology.

A world gone insane is a good place for Zen to grow.

Zen enriches whatever it touches, whether it be art, making tea, or cutting your opponent in two.

Some say that Zen is madness in the midst of sanity, but really it is sanity in the midst of madness.

Soften the glare and untangle the knots, let your cartwheels follow old ruts.

Tao Te Ching

Why sit in ancient temples reeking of incense? Run naked in the fields if you wish. Zen is not to be constrained.

For centuries Zen and Buddhism were like an old married couple. Now they are amicably divorced and share custody of the children.

It is said the books on Zen are like legs on a snake. On the other hand millipedes seem to manage quite well.

Eventually you eat and breathe Zen, but you stop thinking Zen.

When you start to meditate you see little monsters leering at you from the floor, but when you learn to turn your Zen gaze on them they run for cover.

Don't keep trying so hard. Zen is about effortless effort. Think about judo and use your weight wisely.

When you meditate, draw the breath right down as though you want it to reach the center of the earth. This is, of course, impossible, but you will find that you are able to do it with a little practice.

You don't have to understand Zen but you must feel it in your bones.

Meditation shows you many wonderful, delightful things — but don't grab them like a greedy child eager for candy. Let them go. They aren't important.

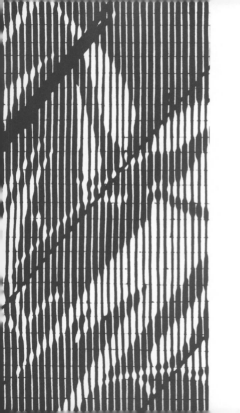

My self long
ago,
In nature
nonexistent;
Nowhere to go
when dead,
Nothing at all.

Ikkyu

Build your tower—construct
it lovingly inch by inch until,
when it is tall enough, lightning
strikes. Wheeee, fireworks!

**They talked of modern art
being the shock of the new.
Zen is the shock of the
ordinary.**

Have you seen those instructions that say, "the parts should just click together— no strength required"? Zen works that way too.

A man once stood in the street trying to give away a gold ingot. He had no success. Teaching Zen is a bit like that.

Zen is about not knowing. Ignorance is something else entirely.

Zen is not some ancient relic to be revered in a museum. It is an axe and only hard use will keep it keen.

With Zen there are no vacations. Not even time for a coffee break. But on the other hand, who needs a break from Zen?

Seek a teacher if you wish, but you will only make progress when you realize that your real master stares at you from the mirror every day.

When you have exhausted all your cleverness you may begin to see what Zen is.

Anyone who tries helpfully to explain Zen to you is doing you a grave disservice.

The task of a Zen teacher is to say, "No. No. No!" until you find the "Yes" for yourself.

Mount Lu in misty rain;
the River Che at high tide.
When I had not been there
how I longed to see them!
I went and I returned.
Nothing special!
Mount Lu in misty rain;
the River Che at high tide.

                    Chinese poem

Pigeons peck at breadcrumbs amidst the melting snow. What would you add? What would you take away?

There is nothing so absurd but that some philosopher has said it.

Cicero

Unless at some time sweat
has streamed down your back
you cannot see the boat sail
before the wind.

Do not avoid life.
Zen is not about
drinking weak tea
in musty parlors.

The nameless
is the origin of
heaven and
earth,
Naming is the
mother of ten
thousand things.

Tao Te Ching

There is a story of a Zen student who cut his arm off to persuade a master that he was sincere enough to become his pupil. Why pay such a price for what is yours already?

All you really need for Zen is insatiable curiosity.

We love to chop things up into little bite-size chunks, but the world must be swallowed whole.

There is not a space as thick as a gnat's eyelash between you and Zen.

When you start Zen is nowhere— later it is everywhere.

Nothing can be added, nothing taken away. Zen is always just right. There is no area of life that Zen cannot enliven with its touch. Your life will gleam like a diamond if only you let it.

Buds
Develop

All religions have, at one time or another, found a Zen of their own — but they quickly bury it again before it upsets things.

Like lightning, Zen strikes all over the globe all the time — but only certain people know they were struck and only some of them do anything about it.

All those Buddhas! Hundreds of thousands all over the world— what a bonfire they would make!

Each day we fritter away our time with meaningless trivia—quite unaware that every bit of garbage and tat is a priceless gem.

Normal life carries on without people noticing just how extraordinary it really is.

Imagine you're an ice block in the sea. You're an individual with a shape, size, and color, but are you really any different from the sea around you?

What would you do with the world? It is far too good to waste.

Forget Japan, forget China, forget, above all, the "Mystic East." Buddha wears jeans.

Those who venerate Buddha know nothing of Buddha. Those who worship Buddha as a god spit on him without knowing.

Religion is taught so badly that people either end up believing a silly fairytale or end up not believing it. What good is that? In either case God gets ignored.

How can something so obvious keep getting missed? It's like the whole world conspires not to see Mount Everest.

I learned to meditate before I'd ever heard of meditation and when someone offered to teach me I thought, "Oh, so *that* is what all the fuss is about!"

In the end you are your own best Zen teacher—accept no substitutes.

Some Zen students are very proud that the teachings they follow have been passed on from one master to another for centuries. They call it their "Zen lineage." Oh, let's have a garage sale—I'm sure that lineage would look just great on someone's desk.

Iron the creases out of your life and smooth your path—you create all those bumps and hollows to trip yourself up.

The moment something becomes difficult or bothersome you know you're doing it wrong. Be here and now. Get rid of superfluous ideas and things will flow smoothly.

"So-and-so called while you were meditating," said my wife. I know. Where does she think I go to meditate—Japan?

"Why don't you go out and have some fun?" my mother used to ask. "All that meditating is so *serious*." Meditation is fun and it gives point to your whole life. Better than a party any day.

If you try to grab life—you'll only scare it away. Like a bird, it will grow tame if you don't threaten it.

Sit quietly and wait. Let things happen as they will and know when to act and when to leave well alone.

Trying to "save" people is a wonderful way to destroy them. Let them save themselves if they must or, better still, let them stay unsaved.

It's no good wishing you were someplace else, doing something else. This is where you are, doing what you have to do. Relax. Do it. Everything else is superfluous.

**Original realization is
marvelous practice.**

Zen saying

The world does not need improving.
You do not need improving. When you
understand that, both you and the
world will be much improved.

At one stroke I forgot all my
   knowledge!
There's no excuse for artificial
   discipline,
For, move as I will, I manifest
   the ancient Way.

                        Hsiang-yen

**Don't tell me you can't find time for
Zen unless you can also say that
you have no time to breathe.**

Zen makes some people very annoyed. That's OK. If it didn't upset them it wouldn't be Zen.

Why can't people leave religion alone and go looking for God instead?

Think of all the centuries, the money, the effort, the tons of stone put into building houses of worship. Didn't they know that God is homeless?

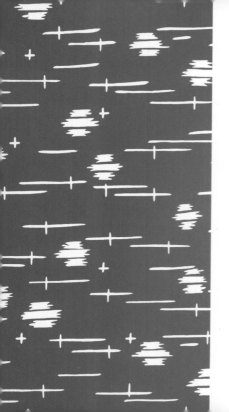

Wherever I hang my hat, that's my home— a *very* Zen thing to say.

I've never taught my kids anything about religion. I'd really hate to spoil it for them.

The seeds of Zen are blowing gently across the earth. What a riot of color we shall see when they germinate! And what a good time to be a gardener.

Writing about Zen, or anything else, is a strange process—it's a bit like sowing seeds and never knowing in what unlikely places they germinated.

You can have Zen the hard way or the easy way. The hard way is very hard and the easy way is very easy. So why do so many people choose the hard way?

People like to ask about *satori* but I don't encourage dirty talk like that.

The wild geese do not mean
to cast a reflection,
The water has no intention
of receiving their image.

Zenrin

Zen is all about thinking dangerously.

You have spent your life absorbing other people's opinions. We all do it. Now throw it all out and learn for yourself.

People feel threatened and rush to the defense of their God—as if God wasn't big enough to take care of Himself.

God is not some king, some angry (or even loving) parent, or some cheap magician full of party tricks. Which is why Zen hardly ever uses the word.

People say, "But what do you *believe*?" As if belief has anything to do with it.

Give something a name and you set limits on it. The name Zen is merely a convenience because you need to call it something. But people tend to confuse the name with the real thing and that can only lead to trouble.

To learn meditation they start you off counting your breaths. It's surprising how many people get confused on the way from one to ten.

Zen may be zany but what is zany is not necessarily Zen.

You can't teach on old dogma new tricks.

Dorothy Parker

When you dance, the object is not to get to the end but to enjoy the moment. Meditation is the same.

I like Buddha even though he always talked too much.

You can be sure that when there is a sudden interest in religion it is not really religion they are interested in.

The world of Zen is strange,
but not half as strange as
a world without Zen.

**I've always found Zen is rather
like finding your way back to the
house you lived in as a child.**

Zen will take care of you
even when you forget to
take care of yourself.

A Zen teacher's job is not to impart information, but to show you that you don't know.

Your mind is as cluttered as an old attic. It is not good enough to tidy the room—you must throw everything out.

Whatever you say about Zen is untrue. What I have just said is therefore also untrue.

Zen students learn that everything they do is meditation. No matter how much they parrot the words, it takes years to learn what they mean.

Anyone who says, "I am a Zen teacher," is to be avoided.

A hermit sitting in his mountain cave may be a good Buddhist, but he knows nothing about Zen.

Your own life is your greatest adventure. What a shame to fill it with TV and beer.

When someone says, "God forbids this!" he means "I forbid it!"

You need no one's permission to contact It. You are It.

The world is full of people who would like to tell you how to live your life. Zen students should turn a cold shoulder to such advice.

It may be that you as a person do not exist, but it is up to you to find that out for yourself.

First you see Zen all around you, then you find it inside you, and then ... pouf!

Buddhism is like the home I grew up in. But, like all grown-up people, there comes a time to leave home.

Zen is grown-up stuff, but very few people are really willing to grow up.

Happily will I sell for profit
Merchants of the town
My hat laden in snow.

Basho

People cherish dreams and illusions.
These are comforting but they
ultimately let you down. Zen is hard
but it never lets you down.

You can only learn Zen like you
learn diving—you jump right in.

When the many are reduced to one what is one reduced to?

Koan

Being a mortal with Zen is better than being a god without.

A Zen master once wrote, "The purpose of Zen is the perfection of character." Baloney! Did he think Zen is concerned with such meager stuff?

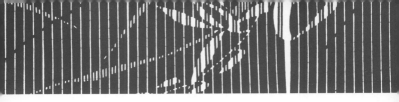

Wash yourself in Zen—let it soak right in. It's no good just wetting the surface.

I stretch lazily and grab handfuls of good Zen air.

I like Zen because
it has no because.

**No way in, no way out, no
way around, over, or under—
where do you go now?**

Grasping Zen is harder than
braiding live eels in a bucket.

A Zen student's interview with the master is formal, intimidating, awe-inspiring. Will he lash out? Are you sure enough to yell, "Kwatz!" right in his face?

When Zen hits you, strike back hard.

"Where are you going?"
asked the boy.
"Where my feet take me,"
replied the other.
"Where are you going today?"
asked the boy.
"Where the wind blows me,"
replied the other.
"Where are you going today?"
asked the boy.
"To the market to buy vegetables,"
replied the other.

**How strange to sit and gabble
about Zen when all the time
you breathe it quite naturally.**

Peter Pan managed to lose
his shadow but his Zen was
fixed more firmly.

**Who would have suspected
that life was all going to
turn out well?**

War, blood, death, and destruction are all very well. But in Zen they wither like dry leaves in an autumn bonfire.

It is said that the Devil sent his daughters to distract Buddha from gaining enlightenment. Fool! He didn't understand anything.

There is nothing very surprising in Zen. If you found chicken in chicken soup would you be amazed?

When Buddha is enlightened the Devil, kicking and screaming, is enlightened too.

To grasp the truth intellectually is not a problem. But to feel it in the marrow of your bones is the difficult part.

With Zen your feet become rooted in the center of the earth and your head reaches the clouds.

Politics is the art of the possible but Zen is the art of the impossible.

Who are we? Where do we come from? Where are we going? Such questions are for children and fools. The children will, with luck, grow out of them.

Stop chattering and listen, listen, *listen*!

You know the answers already, but you have to know that you know them.

There is nothing strange and mysterious about Zen. The only odd thing is the way people fail to understand the obvious.

No matter how much you understand, you do not understand at all.

Zen won't make you walk on water or fly through the air, but who needs it? A bit of grass can float and any bug can fly. Zen is about more important stuff than that.

One glimpse of Zen and everything is Zen as far as the eye can see.

You don't need gods, angels. or little green men from Alpha Centauri.
All you need you already have.

Some people believe that God's power flows through them like electricity through a lightbulb. But supposing God was not only the power but the bulb as well.

The less there is me, the more there is Zen. The more there is Zen, the more there is me.

It's no good trying to get rid of your ego by being meek, obedient, and self-effacing. These things are just the reverse face of the same old ego.

Ego flows out quite naturally as Zen flows in.

It's no good trying to be good, kind, and virtuous unless that is how you feel. The world has enough hypocrites. Let Zen fill you up and morality will take care of itself.

So many hells constructed painstakingly out of people's good intentions.

God is very obliging and will wear whatever mask you desire. Only in Zen are all masks laid aside.

Let's go to war! Let's kill the unbelievers, terrorists, and foreigners. It's what God wants, after all. Doesn't He?

If you see a world of disaster and strife you are not paying attention.

Once you have glimpsed the tail of the bull, finding the head is no great task.

"I am not your friend," Master Shunryu Suzuki is supposed to have said to a sobbing student. Now that's a *real* friend.

Look out!
It's behind you!

Fruit Ripens

Forget all idea of separation. There are never two, only One.

Meet a devil and pat his head—how will he stop being a devil without your help?

Meditation will make you open, kind, and generous. These qualities will help your meditation.

If you have life now and understand what it is, why seek enlightenment?

Don't keep looking for something that is Other, look only for that which is your own.

Grain and flour are not two things but two aspects of one thing. God and humans are like that.

Why were so many of those old Zen masters so grumpy? Zen has plenty of room for laughter.

Take all the rules, the Noble Eightfold Path, and the precepts and scatter them all to the winds. Then watch those winds. Wheeeeeee!

I like words. Give me a crossword puzzle and I'm happy. But words are only toys, they aren't good for anything serious.

Birth and death, coming
and going—what a joke!

**No one knows the final word.
"Magnificent" comes close.**

Eat, sleep, make love—
life is just as it looks.

Psychologists, philosophers, physicists, mathematicians, and all the others love to have theories—but life is not a theory and cannot be contained by theories. Throw away your books and let life happen to you.

Try, try, try, and, when that doesn't work, let go, let go, let go.

Zen adapts itself. The Zen of medieval Japan is as much use to us as a rusty old sword.

Unless your Zen works in downtown New York, or London, or some place no one ever heard of in the backwoods of Vermont, *it ain't Zen*!

Once you have Zen everyone you look at becomes enlightened.

It took years to unlearn things I knew— and even now there are things I think I know and have to struggle to remind myself that I don't.

A precious jewel lost in the mud is still a precious jewel. Zen is there whether you know it or not.

You think that if you let go you're going to fall, but in fact you rise like a helium balloon.

Zen is quite, quite safe. You won't lose your mind (in the traditional sense), but you'll lose that great lump of muck you've been carrying around where your mind was supposed to be.

Zen is like a tiger—once it has your scent it will hunt you down.

People worry that Zen looks difficult. It's actually easy but they can't grasp how easy, so they convince themselves it must be hard.

It's fun to kick the walls down. Crash, bang, wallop! The light flows in everywhere.

Zen is waterproof, shockproof, unbreakable, legal, nonfattening, organic, and has no genetically modified ingredients. Oh yes, it's also *free*. So what's stopping you?

Let's throw a Zen party and invite our friends. Afterward we'll all help Buddha do the dishes.

If I could say just one thing about Zen it would be, "jalapeño."

If you can't get it, throw it out.
Then you'll have it.

**Even if the earth crashes into the
sun and the stars fall from the sky
Zen will continue. If it didn't it
would not be Zen.**

A Zen poem: "Moon."

Let's play a game. I'll go hide under Zen and you try to find me.

I ate too much Zen and now I keep bringing up *koans*.

Turn upside down and then, *very carefully*, balance the earth in both hands.

People persist in wanting things they can't have, even though they already have everything.

Throw out husbands, wives, and children—let's get to know these people properly.

While you know above from below, left from right, before from after— you are a slave to convention.

All the time, no matter what you do, no matter whether you want it or not, Zen is pumped into your lungs.

Everything that people try to split apart, Zen immediately joins back together.

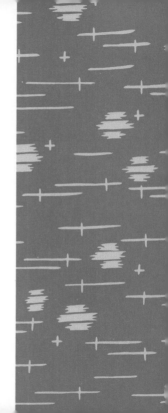

Like spontaneous combustion, Zen burns you up from the inside when you least expect it.

Many people hate Zen because it looks like it may make other people happy without permission.

Stop those stupid thoughts going around and around. Keep still and they'll swim away to feed elsewhere.

Every resident of hell is
provided with a key and
a "get out of jail free" card.

**Hurry! Hurry!
Enlightenment is on
sale right now. Get
yours while stocks last!**

Like the Pied Piper,
Zen leads you on a
merry dance.

**When I was little I wanted
Zen but my mother said I'd
forget to clean out its cage.**

Some people think I say silly things to annoy them. Well, I'm tempted, but the truth is that saying sensible things would do them no good at all.

**Even in darkest winter,
Zen makes flowers bloom
everywhere you look.**

What does it mean?
Nothing *means*
anything.
Everything just is.

Zen doesn't mind what you eat, what hat you wear, or whether you washed your hands before meditating. Just do it.

Looking at Zen is a little like looking at the Grand Canyon—it's hard to get your head around the whole thing all at once.

It doesn't matter who you are or what you've done, Zen is available to you if you want it. You don't even have to say "sorry."

What was the Big Bang? A scientist stubbed his toe on reality.

Better madness than mathematics!

You can't worship Zen, praise it, or love it. You just have to *do* it.

In Zen you become
all new and shiny.

**Any fool can complicate matters—
the trick is to simplify.**

Sometimes there is nothing
you can say. I wish I could
give you this silence.

**Even if you don't know what Zen is, there
is nothing to stop you from finding it.**

A famous nineteenth-century atheist used to challenge God to strike him dead. Challenge Zen and it will shock you into life.

If your Zen excludes even the tiniest particle of the universe it is not Zen.

If you can breathe you can do Zen. If you can't you may consider yourself excused.

Once I could only experience Zen sometimes, if I felt good. Now I know that it's there all the time, no matter how I feel.

Anyone can like nice, good-natured people. But nasty people are Buddhas too. If you can't get your head around this your Zen is not yet ripe.

Zen makes you accepting of other people, even if they are not accepting of you.

Zen has no quarrel with any religion. Some paths may look strange to us but not to those who walk them.

Zen talks of nonattachment but, in the end, how can you possibly be detached from anything?

The English don't like music.
They just like the noise it makes.
Sir Thomas Beecham

**All talk of Zen is only a shadow
of an approximation. Zen itself
has to be experienced.**

If Zen is for you then you'll find your
way, even though your path lies
through great peril. If it's not for you
then you won't even find the path.

It is when there is nothing left to say that Zen becomes most eloquent.

Just because Zen is hard to grasp does not mean it doesn't exist. Water is hard to grasp, but it keeps you alive, doesn't it?

The point in Zen is not to believe anything in particular but to look unflinchingly at what is there.

If you want Zen then you must forget all those "religious" concepts. Faith, and God, and sin, and redemption are all fine but they have nothing to do with Zen.

People try to force life into molds of their own making. Why should life wear a corset?

Members of other religions can practice Zen (after all you only have to sit on your butt and breathe)—but you need to be willing to let it happen to you, even if "it" is not what you were expecting.

Why is it dangerous to walk over a rickety bridge? Because you are attached to the concept of danger and falling. Once your mind is free the bridge is no longer rickety.

It's no good whining to Buddha to help you. Buddha's dead. But if you grab Zen and hold on tight you'll find that you have power you did not understand before.

There is no outside to your mind. Everything is in your mind because, if it weren't, you would be unaware of it.

Take control. You wouldn't let someone bully you in your own house, so why should you be shoved around in your mind?

Of course, there's another thing to think about: Are you sure that "your" mind is really yours?

You do not have to understand Zen. You don't need qualifications in religion or psychology or philosophy—all you need is the spirit of a true explorer to go out and find whatever is there.

How many things do you believe because other people told you about them? Hundreds? Thousands? Millions? Zen is one thing that you need to find for yourself, but it affects all the others.

People want to believe in something but are not able to swallow "three impossible things before breakfast." Zen lets you find out for yourself.

I'd like to give you Zen but I can't. It doesn't work like that. You have to go and get your own.

My friend said, "I'm just skeptical about this Zen business." What, you can't sit on your backside or you can't breathe?

Zen Buddhism (as opposed to Zen) has sutras, and prayers, and candles, and drums, and incense. But all these are just props. The play can be performed perfectly well without them.

Whenever you come across a Zen Center be sure that you won't find the center of Zen there.

Zen has an important role to play. Don't waste time playing dressing-up games. Would you have a water fight with your friends if people were dying of thirst?

Zen isn't a social club. If you want to make friends and influence people go join the Shriners (you even get to wear a funny hat).

Zen was brought here with great care and effort so that you could use it. The question is, what are you going to do with it now?

Each generation adds to Zen. Each master has some new slant to offer. But do not be sentimental about the past—Zen is meant for hard use.

Buddhists have long suspected that Zen was never really a school of Buddhism. Of course, they were right. Zen is a wolf in Buddhist's robes.

You know about grandpa's axe? It's had seven new handles and three new blades but we still call it grandpa's axe.

When she was little my daughter liked to ride on my shoulders and, reaching around, would tweak my nose hard. Zen has a similar sense of humor.

Sometimes I talk as if Zen were alive, almost a person or a god. But that's not right. On the other hand it is by no means a dead thing.

There is a sense in which Zen, like a good dancing partner, responds elegantly, gracefully to your every move.

When I first read about Zen I wanted more than anything to understand it, but I couldn't. However, wanting was enough. Eventually it found its way over, around, and under my mental block.

A world so in love with blood and fire has little time for Zen. Aren't we lucky that Zen has so much time for the world?

Zen is not a game, though it can be surprisingly playful.

You want to know what Zen looks like? Without using a mirror try to see the place at the back of your head.

Once Zen seemed remote, distant, vague. Now it is as real and urgent as a lover's embrace.

Searching for Zen is like an old man using his spectacles to hunt for his spectacles.

What is objectivity? If I say I see a flower and you say it's just a chocolate wrapper, why should I believe your "objective" opinion? After all, you're in my mind too.

There is no right place to start on Zen, just like there is no right place to start on a plate of spaghetti— just jump in anywhere.

People are scared that enlightenment might make them different. You'd think they'd be more scared of staying the same.

Zen doesn't turn you into someone else, it just makes you more you.

Zen shines on everyone, but most people keep out of the sun.

**People think they have a little mind
in their head and a big one that
knows the world outside.
These two are the same—
they just have different names.**

When you dig a deep
enough hole, water
fills it. When you dig it
in yourself, Zen fills it.

I like Zen because it is so unfussy. It's like getting rid of Aunt Mildred's chintzy furniture and getting some Shaker chairs instead.

If there are things about Zen you don't understand that's OK. No one said you had to do it all today.

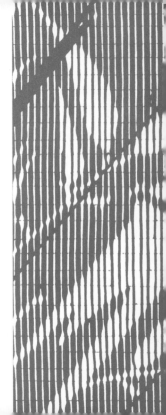

Intellectual understanding is simply not the point. You can't have theories about Zen—you can only feel it as it soaks through your skin.

Some scientific people like to call Zen "mystical nonsense," which is an excellent description. Pity that they don't understand what it means.

If you think that Zen is somehow all tied up with tarot cards, *I Ching*, crystals, and *feng shui* you're in for a shock. Zen is as similar to those things as a tiger is to a hamster.

You can soon spot people who are on the Zen path because, even if they don't yet know it themselves, they question "reality" and are asking the right questions.

Someone asked me to visualize my future—a long, straight road goes on and on.

Even as a Protestant child in Scotland,
I never managed to feel like a miserable
sinner in need of salvation. I felt like an
adventurer on a long journey.

Listening to Zen masters
is rather like reading a sex
manual while making love.

Just when you show people how to soar like swallows, they insist on dabbling like ducks.

Buddhism without Zen is like Coke without bubbles. Zen without Buddhism is like a bird without a cage.

Zen has been battered by Buddhists and neutered by New Agers. It's high time it was allowed to flourish unhindered.

Let's plant Zen seeds and stand astonished as the flowers come up.

Even the best religion (and Buddhism gets my vote) is only a pale, insipid, hampered version of the truth.

There are no rules in Zen except that you keep exploring. If you think you've reached your destination you haven't.

Why did the masters of old eschew everything that was fun in life? Zen that cannot encompass every single thing is not Zen at all.

On receiving a stupid answer
the master Huang-po gave his
student a slap. "How uncouth
you are!" shouted the student.
"What a fool to distinguish
between couth and uncouth,"
replied Huang-po and gave
him another slap.

Every breath you take fills you with enlightenment.

Zen is better than sitting around doing nothing.

You are what you think.

We want to be good at Zen.
We have "good at" minds.
But Zen is not like chess or
soccer or bowling. You
can't be a champion. If your
Zen is plain, simple, and
honest, like homemade
bread, then it will be good.

Better than sovereignty over the earth, better than the heaven state; better than dominion over all the worlds is the first step on the Path to holiness.

Dhammapada

Better break both legs than take such a step.

That Buddha is a tricky fellow, always trying to fool people with his robes and his holiness.

If your meditation leaves you with a special feeling that you think is Zen, throw it out.

A state of *samadhi* is not hard to attain in quiet solitude. If you can do it in Grand Central Station or Trafalgar Square you're getting somewhere.

"What is my self?"
"What would you
do with a self?"
"Am I right to say
I have no idea?"
"Throw away that
idea of yours!"
"What idea?"
"You're free, if you
wish, to carry about
that useless idea of
no idea."

A monk asked, "Why did the First Patriarch come from the west?" "Pass me that board," requested the master. Then he hit him with it.

I like Daruma's fierce tiger gaze. Ask him a question and you take your life in your hands.

My friend Yukiko read me a *haiku*. "I really liked that one," I said.
"Did it make you feel cold?" she replied.
"No."
"In that case you didn't understand it."

Zen takes you over little by little. All you have to do is say, "Yes!"

Juice
Flows

Give me your Zen!
You've had it long
enough and done
nothing but keep it
under the bed to
gather dust.

Zen needs people who are alive, and passionate, and who dare to think dangerously. Most Buddhism is as dangerous as a church social, but less interesting.

An old English Buddhist lady once confessed to me that, deep inside, she'd found she was "not a very nice person." Clearly more digging was required.

It can make you impatient watching people miss the point. It's like being an adult at a children's game of Blind Man's Buff.

Meditate as often and as sincerely as you can. Aside from that, *live*. You won't find Zen by shutting life out.

Just occasionally it's good to look back down the road and see how far you've come.

In Buddhism people are born again and again. Until they find enlightenment they are condemned to a world of sorrow, pain, and death. But hang on. If they go around and around, why aren't they enjoying a world of birth, renewal, youth, and beauty?

It is not fair to blame people who don't understand simply because it is hard to understand. The ones I despise are those who don't understand, but use their ignorance to enslave others.

If anyone tells you God commands you to do this or that, tell him to get lost — God knows your address.

It isn't that any particular religion is wrong, it's just that all of them peddle second-hand experience. If you want the real thing you have to get it for yourself.

In a synagogue I was asked to cover my head, in a church to bare it, and in a temple to take off my shoes. Can God really be so interested in my head and feet? Or does this sound like someone who should get out more?

Why would people rather have a phoney spirituality full of plaster saints and so-called miracles than the real thing?

There used to be some graffiti that said, "95 percent of everything is crap." That was true, but the percentage was, perhaps, on the low side.

The samurai who spent much of their lives in gruesome and bloody battles took Zen to their hearts. Those who embrace milk-and-water Zen should ponder this.

I would love to pick the world up and give it a good shake—not because I hate it, but because I love it so.

When Zen gets you it's rather like being a flashlight bulb that's been accidentally plugged into an electrical outlet. Only this bulb doesn't burn out.

At twenty, and without Zen, I had the heart of a fifty-year-old. Once you find Zen you just get younger all the time.

See you not that easygoing man of Tao, who has abandoned learning and does not strive?
He neither avoids false thoughts nor seeks the true,
For ignorance is in reality the Buddha nature,
And this illusory, changeful, empty body is the Dharma body.

Cheng-tao Ke

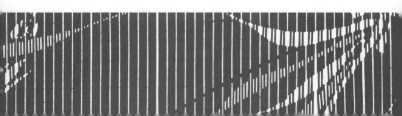

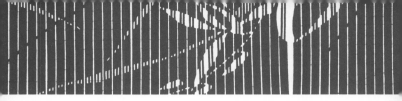

Birds sing, flowers grow, bugs fly hither and thither in the spring sunshine. Where is Buddha while all this is going on?

**The morning glory that blooms
for one hour
Is no different from the
mountain pine
That lives for a thousand years.**

Zen poem

He who lives out his days has had a long life.

Taoist saying

Where would Buddhism have been without the Taoists? They gave it such a kick in the butt that it hiccupped and produced Zen.

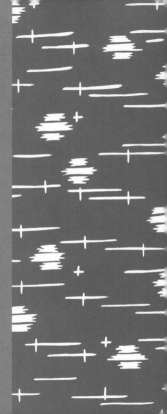

A world without Zen is as likely as a thirsty fish.

Don't tie yourself up in knots thinking about Zen. Thinking is not the point. Just let your thoughts flow as they will.

We passed a field full of scarlet flowers and my Thai girlfriend shouted joyfully, "Look! Puppies!"

A fallen flower
Returning to the branch?
A butterfly!

As when traveling in misty mountains, there is no way to see the end of your Zen journey.

With every step you take you reach your goal.

You can't see Zen in the same way an ant can't see an elephant.

You stand less chance of giving up Zen than the mouse does of giving up the cat.

Being consumed by a cat is to be avoided. Being consumed by Zen is actively to be sought.

Zen isn't about old men behind monastery walls—it's about you and you and you.

Don't waste time thinking too much about Zen—that's like a bird wondering about air.

Every generation gets a chance to make what it will of Zen. What will ours do?

Never
before in the
history of
the world
has Zen
been known
to so many.
The
possibilities
take my
breath away.

What is known as the teaching of Buddha is not the teaching of Buddha.

Diamond Sutra

When you study Zen it's a bit like putting a nesting box in your backyard. It may be a very nice box and you may have taken a lot of trouble with it, but whether the birds come to nest in it is not your decision.

Why is the world full of illusions? Who knows? Maybe it's more fun that way.

**Reason is like an officer when the
   king appears;
The officer then loses his power
   and hides himself.
Reason is the shadow cast by God;
   God is the sun.**

Jalal-udin Rumi

The children of God are very dear but very queer, very nice but very narrow.

Sadhu Sundar Singh

When tired while meditating, take a nap. You think snoozing isn't Zen too?

Don't beat yourself up over Zen (and don't let others do it for you.) Take your Zen gently.

Think about this: Does your Zen improve your life, does it make those around you happier? If not, you're doing something wrong.

If you would swap your Zen for a lottery win, then it wasn't really Zen you had.

Like the blind men who could not agree on the shape of the elephant, we each experience Zen in our own way.

Much religion spends its time hiding from life and building walls to keep it out. Kick down the walls and take a walk.

A new teacher arrived and rearranged the cushions in the meditation hall. The students were in an uproar. Stupid teacher, stupid students! Zen is about much more than cushions.

Don't waste your life on things that don't matter. Anything *can* be Zen, but only if you approach it in a Zen manner.

**A career in Zen is a life wasted.
Teach no more than you have to.
When you've finished — shut up!**

If you struggle against greed or anger or
lust, you are letting these things disturb
you. You are letting them make lumps in
your thinking. Let your thoughts come
and go. Squash those lumps.

Trust your mind. You don't have to ride shotgun to make sure it doesn't misbehave.

I have met no evil people, but many foolish, weak, and stupid ones. The consequences of these failings can be drastic. When your life is in a hole— stop digging!

People who go wrong tangle themselves up in life, like a kitten in a heap of wool. Avoid the tangles at all costs!

Sell your
cleverness
and buy
bewilderment;
Cleverness is
mere opinion,
bewilderment
is intuition.

Jalal-udin Rumi

A friend told me that, one day, scientists will discover what causes the Zen "brain state" and will be able to put it in a pill. Yeah, and they'll have pig flying pills as well.

Sometimes *satori* comes after a period of intense effort. That's fine, but it will still be unripe. Better to take your time. Who needs green apples?

If you approach Zen with ideas of gain you'll never understand it. There *is* nothing to gain—you've got it already.

Learning that enlightenment is not the be all and end all of Zen is the most important step to enlightenment.

The old masters talked of Zen in terms of strenuous effort, but it's much more like something you relax into.

Zen requires a special sort of relaxation. Normally when you relax enough you go to sleep. In Zen you must learn to relax while remaining watchful.

Perhaps Zen is like a game of hide-and-seek. When you finally find yourself, you cry out with delight.

Your secret fearing, longing self is deep as the ocean. Imagine Zen as a powerful dye slowly coloring it all. It takes a long time to plumb the depths.

**Man is made by his belief.
As he believes so he is.**

Bhagavad Gita

In Zen you don't have to repent, beg forgiveness, or promise to reform. All you need to do is cast off your false self and find the real one waiting beneath.

My kids tease me for being old. I tease them back and say it was only when I hit fifty that I started to ripen. But Zen feels that way.

Once each day seemed more or less like every other day. Now each day is a new adventure.

I like to cook. I could never understand those old ladies who had a good recipe and kept it secret. If I have a good one you're welcome to it. Sharing is half the fun. Sharing Zen is fun too.

There is no reason why the world cannot be an excellent place to live. But trying to poke it, prod it, and force it into shape won't work. It's we who are wrong, not the world.

A colleague once told me that these eastern religions that try to make people live in harmony with the world are OK, but a more exciting idea is to change the world. And did he? Of course not.

Improved medicines, transportation, computers, and so on are fine. But they don't really hit the spot. If I live to 100 with the body of a thirty-year-old but don't realize myself through Zen, I'll have been wasting my time.

We can make medicines and plagues, computers and smart bombs, transportation and missiles. People are like that— they can't resist being clever whatever the cost.

Learning to love your enemies always sounds hopelessly idealistic, but it isn't really. One thing your enemies do is to show you yourself through a distorting glass. It can be an informative experience.

Destruction is, of course, part of the equation. No birth without death, no growth without decay. But let's not go crazy. Wiping ourselves out spoils the game entirely.

They say, "Better the devil you know than the devil you don't," and that's right. Devils make good teachers. Once you know how evil works—which is not always as simple as it sounds—you know what to avoid.

Each time I sit to write about Zen my mind is blank. I don't have an idea what to say. But I need 100 ideas to keep up with my quota. And, lo! 100 ideas pop into existence.

People tell me Zen is all in my mind. Of course it is! Who else's mind would it be in?

437

Just because you can't see, touch, or taste Zen, that doesn't make it nonexistent. It's hugely powerful but, like the sea, it only occasionally shows its power, preferring mainly to stay silent.

I used to hate Sundays. They reminded me of my childhood in Scotland—a going-to-church-in-your-Sunday-best sort of day. Then I realized there were no Sundays, there was only an idea called Sunday—so I threw it out.

Detaching people and things from the ideas we have about them is hard. But it's important to see through the masks. If you mistake the idea for reality you'll let yourself in for trouble, but once you recognize a mask then it becomes just a harmless theatrical prop.

People are happy about getting rid of bad ideas like suffering, pain, grief, and anger. But they hang on to the "good" ones like love, trust, loyalty, and truth. In the end they are all just lumps in your thinking. Lumpy thinking is about as much fun as lumpy mashed potato.

You remember the girl in the fairytale? Every time she spoke a snake or a toad would pop out of her mouth. Maybe she was trying to lecture on Zen.

The Irish have a lovely phrase. They say, "It's like trying to round up mice at a crossroads." That sounds very Zen.

Once on TV they showed a Zen monk approach his master. When asked the answer to his *koan* he tried to growl like a lion. My father—a traditionalist—snorted in derision. But, of *course*, he looked ridiculous— it was the wrong answer.

Zen isn't about having the gift of the gab. Just because you always have something to say does not mean that it will be the right thing. You have to know instinctively what the right thing is.

My friend left school and started to dig a hole. At first it was just a hole, but as he got further down he began to take a pride in it. By the time he'd disappeared from view it was his hole and woe betide anyone who criticized it. We haven't seen him for years.

I'm going to take a walk around the garden. You think I'm cheating you and there are now only 999 paths in the book? If you think that you haven't understood any of them.

A friend asked, "In your Zen where do you go when you die?" There is nowhere to go.

A Muslim friend said, "In my religion you must be ritually clean before you pray." In Zen you never get dirty.

Why write books on Zen when it speaks volumes for itself?

Give people even the tiniest chance and they will run off with the wrong idea about Zen.

There have been experiments to measure the brain waves of monks engaged in Zen meditation. Could anything be more pointless?

If you walked through a baseball crowd would you have any doubt who they were cheering for? Yet people can listen endlessly to talk of Zen and have no idea what is being said.

Sometimes it's tempting to talk about Zen plainly, but you have to check that impulse. It would only confuse matters further.

A friend was making fun of the Buddhist mantra, "Om mani padme hum." "You don't really think that nonsense works, do you?" Well, of course it works, but then so would "Coca-Cola" or "I like Mrs. Wagner's pies." The point of a mantra is not what you say but how long you keep saying it.

Theists mean well, but they are always standing in the light and casting strange shadows on the wall.

Buddha's been dead for 2,500 years and still people pester him for favors and ask him to solve their problems.
Haven't they been listening?

Some friends took me to see one of Buddha's footprints. It was a couple of yards long and had toes all the same length. They were certain it was genuine.

I don't really want to argue about science. I'm just irritated by people who find life so overwhelming that they have to run away and find a "rational" explanation. Anything will do, however stupid, as long as it masquerades as "rational."

I also love the ones who say, "Life could not have evolved on this lump of rock, it must have come from a passing comet, or maybe some other planet." So why is some other lump of rock or heap of ice more likely than this earth?

I love those people who insist, "Man is just an animal." What does this mean? Just because we emerged from the sea, why shouldn't we reach for the stars?

Life is the biggest miracle any of us will ever experience. It would be a pity if you missed it through hiding under the bedclothes.

To my astonishment, the first time I came across the word Zen I knew it was for me. Maybe I just liked the word, but I think not. That moment was like love at first sight and I've stayed faithful ever since.

One day, my colleague said, "This Zen craze will be over and you'll have to find something else to write about." Craze? Zen, even in its current form, has lasted many hundreds of years, so even if a few people lose interest, it is hardly likely to fade away.

The world separates things into little bits: this and that, here and there, right and wrong. Zen, like a huge snake, swallows its food whole.

Can I explain the Friend to one to whom He is no Friend?

Jalal-uddin Rumi

Keep your room simple and empty.
Don't clutter the place with mess.

Do just what you have to do
without fuss. That's enough.

If you are not absolutely convinced
that Mind is Buddha, and if you are
attached to forms practices and
meritorious performances, your
way of thinking is false and quite
incompatible with the Way.

Huang Po

When you breathe nothing but pure Zen, you will know.

If you are pulled violently here and there by likes and dislikes, how will you find the Way?

Have you heard the story of the man who kept banging his head against the wall. He said he did it because it was so nice when he stopped.

Such as men themselves are, such
will God Himself seem to them to be.

John Smith, the Platonist

It is said that even after Buddha
became enlightened some people
mocked and criticized him. That's
just people for you. If you're
interested in Zen you have to be
prepared for critics.

Any flea as it is in God is nobler than
the highest of the angels in himself.

Eckhart

All this God stuff and Buddha stuff is very wearisome. Just breathe deeply instead.

History is more or less bunk.

Imagine the vast ocean. Pick a wave, give it a name, watch it grow and prosper, mourn bitterly for its demise. Stupid or what?

Why not follow the path?
It's a nice life for a walk.

Once you have had the merest taste of Zen you can't stop until you've eaten the whole thing.

You can't find Zen?
When was the last
time you had it?

Like your car keys, Zen is always in the last place you look for it.

Sit down and let your mind go. Don't mess around with it, just let it settle gently of its own accord. How hard was that?

All those Buddhas and patriarchs,
how the sword twitches in my hand!

**If Buddha comes to your door
give him the price of a coffee
and send him on his way.**

Enlightenment is no state. The Buddha
did not attain it. Sentient beings do not
lack it. It cannot be reached with the
body nor sought with the mind. All
sentient beings are already in one form
with enlightenment.

Huang-po

Throw away the books, abandon cleverness, and *look, taste, feel, listen*. This world is not a matter for theories.

People like to draw straight lines. They fit a net over the world to measure longitude and latitude. But the world is wiggly, slippery, and not to be measured or confined.

A frog on a lily pad knows more about meditation than most Zen students.

"I have built many temples and monasteries," the Emperor told Daruma. "I have copied the sacred books of Buddha and supported numerous monks and nuns.
Now what is my merit?"
"None at all," was the reply.

What we call evil is simply ignorance bumping its head in the dark.

Henry Ford

Imperturbable and serene the ideal
    man practices no virtue;
Self-possessed and dispassionate
    he commits no sin;
Calm and silent he gives up seeing
    and hearing;
Even and upright his mind abides
    nowhere.

Hui-neng

Sometimes the masters of old would say, "If you can't get enlightened you'd better kill yourself." Naturally it worked, but what sort of enlightenment is that?

In our life we see only surfaces, but Zen is the inside of everything.

Nothing lasts, everything changes— Zen, however, is always there. Do not try to grasp things or people but look for the Zen that is already yours.

Beware altered states of consciousness. These can be wonderful but they are not Zen. When you find Zen it is like seeing your face in a mirror.

This very earth is the
   Lotus-Land of Purity,
And this body is the
   body of Buddha.

Hakuin

You work Zen, play Zen, eat Zen, drink Zen, make love Zen, and die Zen. What else is there?

Now toss this book aside and find your own Zen—
I've lent you mine long enough.

Published by MQ Publications Limited
12 The Ivories, 6–8 Northampton Street
London N1 2HY
Tel: 020 7359 2244   Fax: 020 7359 1616
email: mail@mqpublications.com

Copyright © MQ Publications Limited 2003

Text © Robert Allen 2003
Design: Philippa Jarvis

ISBN: 1-84072-561-3

3 5 7 9 0 8 6 4 2

Printed and bound in China